The Arty Fact Book

The Arty Fact Book

Gary Panton

Welcome to
ARTY FACTS!

You can see art everywhere you go!
It's in galleries and museums, but it's
also in your home, in parks, in schools
and libraries and even on the street.

But how much do you know about
the art that surrounds you? There are
amazing stories behind some of our
best-known paintings . . . and also some
of our least known!

Some works of art are created by wacky geniuses, and others by dark, tormented talents. Some artists have become even more famous than the work they created, because of the weird and wonderful methods they used.

Where else but the art world can you find secret codes, bitter beefs, sneaky heists, mysterious myths and even some very talented animals?

Get ready for some awesome
– and very arty – facts!

DID YOU KNOW?

For almost as long as there have been humans, there has been art! One etching of a zigzag pattern found on a clamshell is over 500,000 years old and some scientists think it's the earliest piece of art ever discovered.

Our prehistoric ancestors used to create cave paintings of the animals they hunted. As there was no paint in those days, they'd use everything from clay, charcoal, animal fat and even blood to make different colours!

Art is one thing that every ancient civilisation has in common. Vikings used to create elaborate wood carvings covered in battling animals, Romans would make highly detailed busts* of their celebrities and the Egyptians made beautiful statues out of solid gold!

*A bust is a sculpture of a person's head and shoulders.
You'll probably have seen busts in your local museum or gallery.

It seems crazy now, but art even used to be part of the modern Olympic Games. Up until 1948, Olympians competed for medals in events including painting, sculpture and music.

PECULIAR PORTRAITS

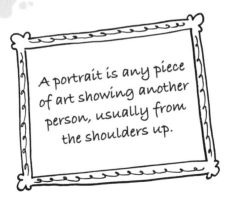

A portrait is any piece of art showing another person, usually from the shoulders up.

The most famous portrait ever made is probably Leonardo da Vinci's *Mona Lisa*. But who was Lisa? Some people think she could be Leonardo himself dressed up as a woman! She's more likely to be Lisa del Giocondo, however, the wife of a rich merchant from Florence.

Another super-famous portrait is *Girl With a Pearl Earring* by Johannes Vermeer. The painting has inspired a novel and even a Hollywood movie, starring Scarlett Johansson from *The Avengers!*

In 1871, artist James Abbott McNeill Whistler painted a portrait of his mum. He called it *Arrangement in Grey and Black No. 1*, but today it's mostly known as "Whistler's Mother". It has featured in *The Simpsons* and the movie *Cloudy With a Chance of Meatballs 2*, and was even once destroyed by Mr Bean!

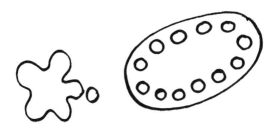

When artists make portraits of themselves, it's called a self-portrait. Self-portraits are the original selfies! A chemist called Robert Cornelius took what has been called "the first-ever selfie" in 1839, by setting up a camera and running in front of it!

Gillian Wearing is another early selfie pioneer! From 1988 to 2005, she took a collection of photos of herself to create a record of her own ageing. More recently, she created digital images imagining how she might look in old age.

Lots of famous people from history have had their portraits painted. Franklin D. Roosevelt, the 32nd President of the United States, collapsed and died while having his portrait taken. The work could never be completed and is now known as *The Unfinished Portrait*.

VINCENT VAN GOGH

Vincent van Gogh lived during the 1800s and is still one of the world's most famous artists, but did you know these arty facts about his life?

As well as being a talented painter, Vincent also loved to write. In a time before emails and messaging he wrote over 800 letters to family and friends, most of them to his brother Theo.

Van Gogh worked on his famous painting *The Starry Night* while staying in a psychiatric hospital in the French town of Saint-Rémy-de-Provence. A wing of the hospital is now named after him.

How busy are you? Probably not as busy as Van Gogh — he created over 900 paintings and over 1000 drawings in his lifetime!

He collected birds' nests and would even sometimes pay local children to gather them for him so that he could paint them.

Would you like to sleep in a painting? Well in 2016 fans of Van Gogh's famous picture *The Bedroom* were given the chance to do just that! The Art Institute of Chicago created a replica of the room shown in the painting, and it was available to rent for just $10 a night.

The story of Van Gogh's missing ear is one of the most famous in the history of art. He chopped it off and gave it to a maid as a gift, but she fainted when he gave it to her!

HARD UP

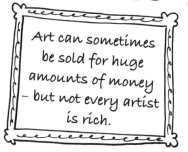

Art can sometimes
be sold for huge
amounts of money
– but not every artist
is rich.

Van Gogh's paintings are worth lots of
money today, so you might think he must
have been loaded, but he hardly sold
any while he was alive. The only one we
can be sure of was *Red Vineyard at Arles*,
which was bought by a friend's sister.

Paul Gauguin, Van Gogh's fencing partner and friend, didn't fare much better. His style changed ideas about painting forever, but he had to take jobs as a stockbroker, sailor and businessman to make ends meet.

Paul Cézanne's paintings are worth a fortune today, but when he died of pneumonia in 1906 he was surrounded by paintings he couldn't sell and bills he couldn't pay.

While living in Paris as a young man, it is rumoured that Pablo Picasso had to burn some of his art to keep his room warm.

Jenny Saville became the highest-selling living female artist in 2018 when her painting, *Propped* (1992) sold for $12.4 million. Previously, this record was held by Yayoi Kusama after one of her Infinity Nets paintings sold for over $7 million in 2014.

French artist Henri de Toulouse-Lautrec didn't just suffer financially. Throughout his life he had health problems and was teased because his legs stopped growing in his early teens and he remained just 4'8" (142 cm) tall.

Johannes Vermeer, who painted *Girl With a Pearl Earring*, had to borrow money throughout his life and left his family in debt when he died in 1675. Over 300 hundred years later and his pictures are some of the most valuable in the world!

As a young man, the great artist Michelangelo buried one of his own sculptures in earth so that it looked older and therefore more valuable. The person who bought it eventually found out he'd been tricked – but let Michelangelo keep the cash because he liked the sculpture so much.

PAUL CÉZANNE

£ $

Of course, not all
great artists had
cash problems!

$ £

French great Paul Cézanne came from
a wealthy banking family and was left a
whopping inheritance from his father (who
had wanted his son to become a lawyer).

Do you know what a "still life" is? It's a painting that shows a collection or display of items, such as fruit and flowers. Cézanne painted loads of them, and, it was reported, he once said of his work "I want to astonish Paris with an apple"!

Tragically, it was Cézanne's dedication to work that killed him. After attempting to work outdoors for hours during a storm, he collapsed, and died of pneumonia a few days later.

In 2011 Cézanne's painting *The Card Players* became the most expensive art piece of all time when it was sold for over $250 million. Turn over the page for more eye-popping sales stats!

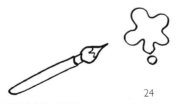

MONEY MONEY MONEY

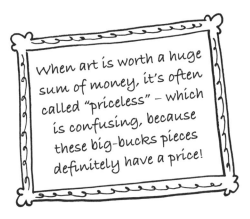

When art is worth a huge sum of money, it's often called "priceless" – which is confusing, because these big-bucks pieces definitely have a price!

The highest price ever paid for a piece of art by a living artist at an auction is $90.3 million, for *Portrait of an Artist* by David Hockney.

The previous record was $58.4 million, for Jeff Koons' *Balloon Dog* (Orange). Despite the name, it's not an actual balloon dog, but a sculpture made from stainless steel.

When a priest took a painting bought for £400 onto the TV programme *The Antiques Roadshow*, it turned out to be worth £400,000! It was a portrait by Anthony Van Dyck, and the priest decided to sell the piece to pay for new church bells.

In 2005, Swiss artist Gianni Motti bought the fat of Italian Prime Minister Silvio Berlusconi from a liposuction clinic. He then turned it into a bar of soap, which he sold for almost £10,000.

Salvator Mundi (which means *The Saviour of the World* in Latin) is, as of 2017, the most expensive artwork of all time. The Leonardo da Vinci painting was sold for a huge $450 million! What do you think about that? Can a painting ever be worth that much money?

When the same painting was sold in the 1950s, it was mistaken for a copy, and apparently changed hands for just $45!

MONET MONET MONET

Claude Monet was one of the great impressionist artists (which means he painted in the impressionist style – not that he was really good at doing silly voices!).

Monet's father disapproved of his career choice as an artist. He wanted him to become a grocer.

Monet started out as an artist in the same way that lots of kids do – by doodling drawings of his teachers! His school notebooks were full of them.

Today, Monet's *Impression Sunrise* is an iconic and world-famous painting, but when he unveiled it in 1874 it was panned by critics and seen as worthless.

No one in history has taken water lilies more seriously than Monet. It is believed that, before painting them, he employed people to paddle out to the lily pads and clean each one individually.

Incredibly, while painting his water lilies masterpieces, Monet could barely see. He had an eye condition called cataracts, and as he grew older it affected his sight badly.

Monet actually created a lot of his best work when his eyesight was at its poorest. Some people think that his eye condition is to thank for the blurry painting style he became famous for!

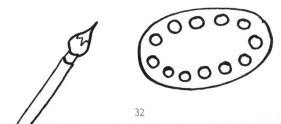

HOT PROPERTY

When art is worth a lot of money,
it is often targeted by robbers.
That's why galleries always need
to have security guards!

When the *Mona Lisa* was stolen in 1911,
one of the main suspects was another
famous artist – Pablo Picasso! He was
even arrested, but was later cleared
of the crime and released.

The actual robber turned out to be one Vincenzo Peruggia — and how did he carry out his masterplan? He simply strolled into the Musée du Louvre (the gallery that owns the *Mona Lisa*) in Paris, lifted the painting off the wall, took it out of the frame and walked out of the building!

Up until then, the *Mona Lisa* wasn't especially famous. It was only after it was stolen, 350 years on from its creation, that it became widely recognised as the masterpiece we know it as today.

In 2015, two brothers sold a fake Francisco de Goya painting for 4 million euros, but the joke was on them – the buyer paid with fake money!

Edvard Munch's *The Scream* is one of the most famous paintings in the world. You might think that the open-mouthed figure is shrieking, but the artist intended to show someone responding in fright to the sound of a scream. There are several different versions of the picture. In 1994, the version kept at Oslo's National Gallery was stolen by two men who broke in and left a note that said: "Thanks for the poor security". It was eventually recovered a few months later.

In 2004, one of the versions kept in the Munch Museum was also stolen. Six men were charged with the robbery, but it took two years for the painting to be found.

While some have tried to sneak paintings out of galleries, one artist was successful in smuggling one in! In 2012, Andrzej Sobiepan took his own painting into Poland's National Museum, waited until the guard wasn't looking, and hung it on the wall! It took three days for it to be noticed and taken down.

PRANKSTER PAINTERS

Do you love a good prank? Then these could be the Arty Facts for you!

During the 1920s, American author Paul Jordan Smith pretended to be a Russian artist called Pavel Jeordanowitch. He made up his own spoof art style, got his work into exhibitions, and even earned the praise of critics. When he came clean in 1927, he said he did it all to prove that art critics don't know what they're talking about!

In 1952, illustrator Hugh Troy placed an advert in a newspaper offering his services as a ghost artist. "Too busy to paint? Call on the ghost artists. We paint it, you sign it," said the ad. Of course, it turned out to be a hoax!

Author William Boyd didn't just create prank art – he created a whole prank artist! He wrote an autobiography of the completely made-up "Nat Tate" (whose name is a combination of "National Gallery" and "Tate"). David Bowie, who was in on the joke, even held a launch party for the book – on April Fool's Day, of course!

Damien Crisp is an artist who loves to make up fake stories. Once he advertised an exhibition of dog paintings by former US President George W. Bush! In fact, Bush really is a keen painter – just not of dogs.

In Switzerland's Art Basel, artist Massimo Agostinelli wrote on a bin, placed it between a couple of exhibits, and stood back while people admired it. The bin later ended up on display in another gallery in Zurich! What do you think about that? Is it art, or just a bin?

ERASER

"Doug and Mikael" are two pranksters who pretend to be art! They've been known to walk into galleries, stand still against a wall, and wait for the art-loving crowds to gather!

While making his TV series "Who Is America?", British comedian Sacha Baron Cohen pretended to be an ex-prisoner who painted with his own poo! He even showed the paintings to an art expert – who later confirmed that the art "stunk".

DAMAGED GOODS

Have you ever accidentally broken an ornament? Imagine if it was a priceless piece of art!

Two vases worth a combined £100,000 were left in pieces in 2006 when a man fell down a staircase in a Cambridge museum and sent them crashing to the floor. He said he was sorry – but was still asked not to return. Oops!

In 2014, a man in Ireland was sent to jail for punching a hole in a Claude Monet painting worth nearly £8 million. He originally said he did it "to get back at the state" – but later changed his story to say that he fell into the canvas by accident.

A cleaner in Rome accidentally threw away two pieces of art worth a combined $13,700 because she thought they were trash. Part of one of the pieces included bits of cookie scattered on the floor – so perhaps it was an easy mistake to make!

Sometimes when art gets damaged there's a happy ending. A plaster statue of Buddha was dropped and the surface damaged, only to reveal that it was made of solid gold underneath.

Le Bateau, a painting by Henri Matisse, wasn't damaged, but it wasn't treated as well as it could have been either! It hung upside-down at New York's Museum of Modern Art for over a month before anyone noticed and put it the right way up.

THIS WAY UP

Hans-Joachim Bohlmann was a vandal who made a lifetime's work out of wrecking valuable art. It's thought that he caused more than 138 million euros worth of damage up until his death in 2009.

An art collector was awarded £350,000 in damages after a storage company mistook an Anish Kapoor sculpture for rubbish and threw it in the bin.

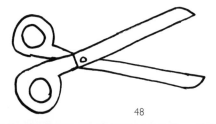

FRIDA KAHLO

Frida Kahlo was a great Mexican artist known for her awesome self-portraits and fascinating life.

Frida Kahlo claimed she was born in 1910, which would be cool as it's the same year as the revolution in her home country of Mexico. The only problem is, she was actually born in 1907. What a fibber.

Kahlo had some really bad luck. As a child, she had the disease polio, which left her with one leg much thinner than the other. In her teens, she was in a bus crash and broke her back, her collarbone, her ribs and her pelvis. Then, in later life, she had to have one foot amputated because of gangrene. She even turned up at her first solo exhibition in an ambulance!

Of the 143 paintings she created, 55 are self-portraits. Perhaps the best known is *The Two Fridas*, in which two versions of her sit next to each other, holding hands.

After she died, her home in Mexico was turned into a museum. Today, over 25,000 art-lovers visit it every month!

MAD METHODS

Not all artists use paint on canvas. There are all sorts of weird and wonderful ways to create art! Check out some of these . . .

Jean-Michel Basquiat liked to wear expensive Armani suits when he painted. He'd then head off on a night out while still wearing them, paint splashes and all.

Jackson Pollock was a famous American artist who created what he described as "drip paintings". It's exactly what it sounds like – he would put canvases on the floor and then drip paint onto them.

Pollock would also take items from around him and add them to his paintings. Cigarette butts, ash and even dead bees can be found on the surfaces of his work!

Tim Knowles is a British artist who creates his art by attaching pens to trees and letting the wind do the work!

Georgia O'Keeffe painted over 200 beautiful close-ups of flowers. She often worked in the desert and had her car customised so that she could work inside it and avoid the scorching sun.

Lucy Gafford, also known as the "Shower Hair Master", creates amazing art out of hair from her shower drain. She then posts photos of her work on social media.

Rice paddy art is where rice is planted in patterns to form incredible visual displays that can only be seen from the air. When the rice is harvested, the amazing art disappears forever.

Willard Wigan is a micro-sculptor. He creates tiny sculptures so small that some can fit inside the eye of a needle. In fact, they're so small that he once accidentally inhaled one!

Viennese artist Gustav Klimt used to cover his sketchbooks in cat urine to preserve his art. Sadly, the smell was so bad that he ended up destroying much of his work.

Artist Sandy Skoglund once filled three rooms from floor to ceiling with different kinds of food: cheese crisps in one, raisins in a second and raw bacon in the third.

On the subject of filling rooms with stuff –
Rachel Whiteread filled a huge hall at the
Tate Modern with 14,000 white boxes.
One of her inspirations was the final scene
of an Indiana Jones movie!

Millie Brown is a "vomit painter" – and yes,
that is as horrible as it sounds! She drinks
coloured milk and throws up to create
works of art that she has sold for thousands
of dollars!

Chris Trueman has an especially gruesome technique – he creates pictures out of dead ants! He used 200,000 of them to create one picture of his brother.

Val Thompson has taken her art a step further — she uses dead people! After they are cremated, she uses their ashes to create her paintings.

Nathan Sawaya is an artist who makes his sculptures out of LEGO® bricks! He's held exhibitions of his work all over the world, and owns over 1.5 million LEGO® bricks!

PAINTING WITH POO

If you found any of the last section disgusting, you might want to skip this part!

English artist Mary Barnes discovered her talent for painting during a stay in a psychiatric centre where she would paint with her own poo! The staff eventually made the wise decision to give her some paint instead.

In 1961 Italian artist Piero Manzoni announced that he was selling 90 tin cans full of poo although some people think they are just full of plaster. Today, the cans are worth over £100,000 each. They are so valuable that they can't be opened to find out the truth!

Even the great Pablo Picasso had a go at poo painting! Supposedly, when his daughter Maya was three, he used her poo in his art for its "unique texture"!

In San Francisco in 2013, there was an entire art show dedicated to art created using animal poo from local farms!

Chris Ofili also favours animal poo in his work. He's an award-winning artist who includes paints with elephant dung in his paintings! He first started doing it after bringing some home as a souvenir from a safari trip.

SUFFERING FOR YOUR ART

Some artists like to go to extremes. Here are some examples you should definitely not try at home!

Chinese artist He Yunchang doesn't do things by halves. Examples of his "extreme performance art" include having one of his own ribs removed to wear as a necklace, and imprisoning himself in quick-drying concrete.

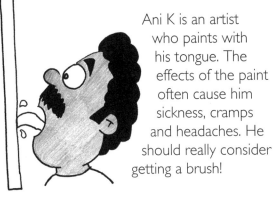

Ani K is an artist who paints with his tongue. The effects of the paint often cause him sickness, cramps and headaches. He should really consider getting a brush!

Chris Burden was another performance artist who was used to a bit of pain. During his life he crawled over broken glass, tied himself to the front of a car, and even had a friend shoot him in the arm.

In 2017, Belgian performance artist Mikes Poppe chained himself to a block of marble and set about trying to chisel himself free. After 19 days of hard work, he gave up and had to ask for help.

Marina Abramovic nearly died during an art stunt that involved setting fire to a wooden star and throwing bits of toenail and hair into it! She had to be rushed to hospital, but thankfully was OK.

AROUND THE WORLD

Here are some crazy Arty Facts from all over the world!

How old do you think you need to be to be a great artist? Not very old at all! Aelita Andre is an Australian artist who has had her paintings displayed in exhibitions since she was just two years old. She held her first solo exhibition at age four!

The Asphaltophone is a musical road created by Danish artists Steen Karup Jensen and Jakob Freud-Magnus. When driven on, vibrations create music that can be heard inside the car. Today, there are also musical roads in Japan, South Korea, the Netherlands and the United States.

Cai Guo-Qiang, from China, uses fireworks to create amazing art, including his Project for Extraterrestrials, which he said was an attempt to speak to aliens.

French artist Yves Klein wasn't happy with the shades of blue available, so created his own, which he called International Klein Blue. He also claimed he could fly!

If you like your art on the unusual side, a trip to Denver Airport in America might be the thing for you. A series of bizarre murals have prompted many conspiracy theories and some people even think the paintings predict the end of the world!

LEONARDO DA VINCI

Painter, sculptor, engineer, scientist, mathematician – was there anything Leonardo couldn't do?

"Da Vinci" wasn't actually his surname – he just used it to avoid confusion with all the other Leonardos working in Florence at the time. "Da Vinci" means "from Vinci", the name of the town in which he was born.

He is said to have been ambidextrous – which means he could use both his right and left hand equally well. It's even been claimed he could draw with both hands at the same time!

Leonardo is best known for the *Mona Lisa*, but another famous painting of his, *The Last Supper*, shows Jesus at a table surrounded by his disciples. The picture originally included Jesus's feet under the table. Unfortunately, in 1652 they were chopped off when builders added a doorway to the wall on which it was painted.

We're lucky *The Last Supper* even still exists! During the Napoleonic Wars, Napoleon's soldiers used it for target practice. Then, during the Second World War, a bomb hit the building it is housed in. Incredibly, the artwork survived.

It is possible that a lost Leonardo masterpiece is hidden behind a wall in Florence's city hall — but the wall can't be taken down to find out, because Giorgio Vasari's priceless *Battle of Marciano* is painted on it.

There are only fifteen confirmed Leonardo paintings still in existance. There would be a lot more, but he had a habit of destroying any of his work that he didn't consider to be perfect.

He was also a designer and inventor. He came up with one of the first ever alarm clocks, and his other designs included a spiky underwater helmet to protect the wearer from sea monsters!

Leonardo wasn't just a great artist and thinker – he was also a great friend to animals. Not content with turning vegetarian, he also used to buy caged birds just to set them free.

HIDDEN MESSAGES

Ever heard of the book and movie called The Da Vinci Code? Well, that story's not really true, but Leonardo did love a secret code!

Vatican researcher Sabrina Sforza Galitzia believes *The Last Supper* contains a "mathematical and astrological puzzle", which predicts a global flood. It will happen in the year 4006, though, so if you're reading this now you should be OK.

In 2011, Italian researcher Silvano Vinceti found something else in the piece – the letters L and V, hidden in the right eye of the Mona Lisa.

It's been claimed that the loaves of bread in the painting actually represent musical notes. They also might just be bread . . .

Leonardo's handwriting can also be tricky to read. He sometimes used backwards "mirror writing" to stop people spying on him and stealing his ideas!

Leonardo isn't the only artist who hid secret codes, predictions and messages in his work. A fifteenth-century masterpiece by Domenico Ghirlandaio shows the Virgin Mary with baby Jesus and St John, but it also includes a strange flying object, which some have claimed could be an alien spaceship!

MYTHS, LEGENDS AND CURSES!

Some paintings tell stories – others have incredible stories that have built up around them!

In 1985, Britain's *The Sun* newspaper organised mass burnings of copies of Giovanni Bragolin's painting *The Crying Boy*. The paper claimed that the picture was cursed, as fire-fighters often found it undamaged in the ruins of house fires.

Another supposedly cursed artwork is *The Hands Resist Him* by Bill Stoneham. An eBay listing in 2000 claimed that the children in the painting could move during the night and even leave the canvas. The page went viral, with some people claiming that even looking at it made them feel unwell.

A spooky painting called *The Anguished Man* is said to be haunted! The owner claims the picture's unknown artist used their own blood to paint it, and ghostly noises can be heard whenever it's on display.

A portrait of a Spanish military leader hanging in a hotel in Texas has also been the subject of some ghostly goings-on. Some of the hotel staff have claimed the eyes of Bernardo de Galvez follow them around the room, and that the painting hates having its photo taken. Scary!

MICHELANGELO

Michelangelo di Lodovico Buonarroti Simoni, or just Michelangelo to his friends, was one of the all-time greats. Here are his Arty Facts!

Michelangelo is best known for painting the Sistine Chapel – but he supposedly hated painting!

While Michelangelo's Sistine Chapel work was still in progress, fellow artist Raphael apparently snuck in to have a look and was so inspired that he went back to one of his own paintings, scraped it off the wall and started again.

When Michelangelo and his assistants painted *The Creation of Adam* on the ceiling of the Sistine Chapel, they did the entire thing standing on scaffolding and looking up while they worked. There's a very good chance they all had sore necks by the time it was finished!

As well as the Sistine Chapel, he's known for his statue of *David* (a hero from the Bible). Two other artists – Agostino di Ducco and Antonio Rossellino, previously owned the marble slab that would eventually become David. Both abandoned it because they decided marble was far too difficult to work with.

Michelangelo may have been a brilliant artist, but his personal hygiene was less impressive. He never bathed, and hardly ever changed his clothes. Pee-yooooo!

ARTY ANIMALS

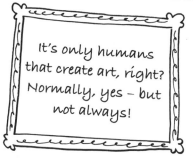

It's only humans that create art, right? Normally, yes – but not always!

In 1964, a Swedish gallery displayed paintings by a mysterious new artist called Pierre Brasau. Brasau's work went down a storm with critics. There was just one important thing they didn't know: Brasau was a chimpanzee.

An even more famous chimp-artist was Congo, who created a staggering 400 works of art during the 1950s. If any of his paintings were removed before they were finished, Congo would throw a tantrum.

In 1974, an art competition run by a Mississippi museum received almost 800 entries – but the winner was a dog! The piece, called *Anitra's Dance*, was basically just a chewed up mitten, but no-one knew the truth until the winner arrived on stage!

Bini is a YouTube star who not only paints, but also combs hair and plays basketball. You might wonder what's so unusual about that – until you discover Bini is a rabbit!

ANONYMOUS ARTISTS

Not all artists want to be famous.
There are some great artists out
there whose identities are closely
guarded secrets.

During the 1400s, an artist in Germany
created incredible prints, engravings and
playing cards which remain in huge demand
to this day. His identity has never been
discovered, so to this day he's known simply
as "The Master of the Playing Cards".

Possibly the strangest character of anonymous art is the "Philadelphia Wireman". In 1982, over 1,000 amazing sculptures made from wire wrapped around household objects were found on a street in Philadelphia. The sculptures have since appeared in galleries and exhibitions all over America – but no one knows who made them.

For the last 20 years, a French artist known only as "Invader" has travelled the world putting up mosaics inspired by the classic video game Space Invaders. His 3,000 pieces have popped up in over 60 different cities. His parents think he works in the construction industry.

Guerrilla Girls is a group of unidentified New York artists who wear gorilla masks and each name themselves after dead female artists, including Frida Kahlo and Georgia O'Keefe.

Anonymous artists don't always stay anonymous forever. For two decades, "Above" was an unidentified artist who travelled the world creating amazing graffiti. In 2017, he finally told us who he was – Berlin-based Tavar Zawacki.

BANKSY

Banksy is one of Britain's most
famous artists working today –
but no one knows who he is!

His graffiti art has popped up all over the
world, but he's somehow managed to
keep his identity completely anonymous.
We do know, though, that he is from
Bristol, works with stencils, and has even
drawn the opening titles to an episode of
The Simpsons.

Here are some more of Banksy's Arty Facts:

He once created fake £10 notes.

Angelina Jolie, Christina Aguilera, Bono and Damien Hirst all own some of his work.

His piece *Bombing Middle England* showed some old ladies bowling with bombs and was sold for over £100,000.

He designed the cover for cover for the Blur album *Think Tank*, an album by the British rock band Blur.

In 2018, Banksy's *Balloon Girl* was sold at an auction for over £1 million – and then immediately shredded in front of the buyer's eyes! Many were shocked – but some have also claimed the whole thing was a hoax!

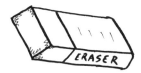

GREAT BRITS

They don't call it Great Britain for nothing! Here are some of GB's finest Arty Facts . . .

Have you heard of J.M.W. Turner? He's one of Britain's favourite artists. He was nicknamed "The Prince of Rocks", because he spent so much of his time painting landscapes!

Turner's painting *The Fighting Temeraire* was voted the country's greatest painting in 2005. It's so popular that it's going to be included on £20 banknotes from the year 2020 onwards.

Turner also has one of art's biggest awards named after him. Every year, the Turner Prize is given to the best artist in Britain awarded to one of the year's best British artists.

My Bed by Tracey Emin is exactly that – her unmade bed! In 1999 it was shortlisted for the Turner Prize, and in 2014 it was sold for over £2.5 million! So maybe it pays not to tidy your bedroom after all!

In 2017, 63-year-old Lubaina Himid became the Turner Prize's oldest ever winner after a rule was lifted that said winners had to be aged 50 or under.

British artist Damien Hirst is best-known for the 14-foot long shark he preserved in a tank and put on display in the Saatchi Gallery in London in 1991. However, in 2006 the original dead shark had to be replaced. A lot of people say it's no longer the same piece of art. What do you think?

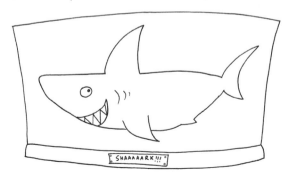

SHAAAAARK!!!

British artist Grayson Perry often includes his lifelong teddy bear, Alan Measles, in his work. Alan is named after a boy who used to live next door to Perry, and measles because the artist caught the illness as a child.

In 2014, Turner Prize winner Catherine Yass wanted to drop a piano from the top of a 27-storey London building "to explore how sound travels". A petition from local residents soon put a stop to that plan though.

The fourth plinth in London's Trafalgar Square has been home to some amazing art. In 2009, over two thousand members of the public were given access to the plinth for one hour each, to do whatever they liked. One person read text messages from the public out loud, one dressed as a football referee and another even pitched a tent!

SALVADOR DALI

Spanish artist Salvador Dali could easily fill a whole book of Arty Facts just on his own! Here are just a few of the best ones.

Dali believed that he was the reincarnation of his dead brother, who was also named Salvador.

He went to art school in Madrid, but didn't stay there very long. He was thrown out before taking his exams, for saying that none o the teachers were good enough to assess him!

He once almost suffocated while giving a lecture in a scuba suit, which had to be prised off him with a billiard cue.

Dali once turned up to an event in a Rolls Royce that he'd filled with cauliflower. He never explained why.

Dali's famous painting *The Persistence of Memory* is known for its melting clocks. He once said he got the idea after watching some cheese melting in the sun.

If you look even more closely at *The Persistence of Memory* you'll also see a group of ants on one of the clocks. Dali included ants in a lot of his work, and it's thought he saw them as representing death and decay. Creepy!

He had a pet ocelot that he used to take out for walks.

Whenever fans asked Dali for an autograph, he would make a point of stealing their pens.

He once set his own bedroom on fire.

In 2017, 28 years after his death, Dali's body was dug up for DNA testing – and it was revealed that his famous upturned moustache was still in tact!

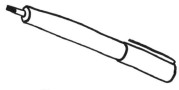

ME, MYSELF & I

For some artists, there's no better subject than themselves! Here are some self-portrait Arty Facts . . .

Rene Magritte painted *The Son of Man* after a friend requested he paint a self-portrait. "We always want to see what is hidden by what we see", said Magritte, whose painting shows a man whose face is hidden by some fruit.

Rembrandt could be called the king of self-portraits. He drew, painted or etched pictures of himself around 100 times. For variety, he often wore different hats and costumes he found in second-hand sales!

Johannes Gumpp painted just one self-portrait, but what a self-portrait it is. He painted himself standing in front of two mirrors, so he appears three times and from three different angles.

Salvador Dali included a portrait or silhouette of himself in all of his paintings — of which there were over 1,500.

Marcel Duchamp created a female alter ego called Rrose Selavy, who featured in many of his paintings. The name is a play on the French phrase *"eros c'est la vie"*, which means "love is life".

Perhaps one of the saddest self-portraits is Pablo Picasso's *Self-Portrait Facing Death*, which he completed less than a year before dying.

Polish artist Rafal Bujnowski came up with a very artistic way of taking a passport photo. He painted a self-portrait, took a photo of it, and used it to apply for an American visa. The application was successful!

RECORD BREAKERS

Biggest, smallest, longest
– here are some of the best
art records!

The world's biggest art gallery and museum
is the Musee du Louvre in Paris. It boasts
38,000 pieces of art – including the
Mona Lisa – and is visited by over
7 million art-lovers every year!

But what about the smallest? A few different places claim that title, but one contender is the gallery in County Durham in England that fits inside a phone box! There's only space for two people, and even then it's quite a squeeze.

Mother Earth, by David Aberg, is the largest picture ever painted by a single artist. It takes up 26,000 square metres, took two-and-a-half years to complete and required 100 tons of paint!

Parimalakanth Kumaravijayan holds the record for drawing the longest continuous line. Stretching over 660 metres, the line includes drawings of sea creatures.

In 2015, people in the Danish city of Copenhagen got together to create the biggest ever piece of chalk pavement art. The final piece took up nearly 20,000 square metres!

You might not have heard of Devwrat Anand Jategaonkar, but he holds a very special world record – in 2017, he built the biggest sculpture ever to be made entirely out of margarine!

PABLO PICASSO

Painter, sculptor, photographer, writer and loads more – Pablo Picasso was undoubtedly one of the greatest artists of the twentieth century.

Picasso may well be the artist with the longest ever name. His full name is Pablo Diego José Francisco de Paula Juan Nepomuceno María de los Remedios Cipriano de la Santísima Trinidad Martyr Patricio Clito Ruíz y Picasso. His friends just called him Pablo.

As a baby, his first word was "*piz*", which is Spanish for pencil.

He hated being asked about the meaning of his paintings. It really, really annoyed him. So he started carrying a gun around so that he could point it at people who got on his nerves. It was full of blanks, but still did the trick.

Picasso was also a passionate animal lover. He had loads of dogs and cats, and didn't stop there. He also had a turtle, a goat, an owl and even a monkey.

When Picasso was asked what the favourite period of his career was, his answer was simple: "The next one."

He hardly ever stopped working, and is said to have carried on painting until hours before his death at the age of 91.

BAD BLOOD

This is what
happens when
artists attack . . .

Michelangelo was disfigured for life after
being thumped on the nose by his mallet-
wielding rival, Torregiano.

Michelangelo also had some serious beef with Leonardo da Vinci. When both were commissioned to repaint the same section of Florence's town hall, Michelangelo spent so much time harassing his rival that the pair had to be separated, and the job was never completed.

Paul Cézanne had a long friendship with the author Émile Zola – but it came to an end when Zola wrote the book *L'Ouevre*, which included a character based on Cézanne. Cézanne wasn't happy, and the pair fell out for good.

Caravaggio was not a man you would want to upset. While enjoying a meal in a restaurant he once smashed his plate into the waiter's mouth. On another occasion, he attacked a fellow painter with a sword because he'd heard that the painter had said something unkind about him.

ARTY CELEBS

Did you know that loads of famous TV and movie stars are also art lovers?

In 2011, Hollywood actor James Franco gave his backing to The Museum of Non-visible Art. None of the art actually exists, which is why it's "non-visible". That still didn't stop someone from paying $10,000 for one of its pieces!

Legendary TV host Bruce Forsyth used to copy the pose of Auguste Rodin's *The Thinker* statue at the start of his telly appearances. You might remember "Brucie" from *Strictly Come Dancing!*

Hollywood actor George Clooney pulled an awesome art prank on his friend Richard Kind. After pretending to be attending art classes, he presented Kind with the ugliest painting he could find, and pretended to have painted it. Kind by name, Kind by nature, Richard pretended to like it and hung it in his house for two years.

When *Red Balloon* by Banksy went on sale at auction, there was an A-list bidding war between Charlize Theron and Coldplay singer Chris Martin! Chris won in the end – and it set him back $650,000.

Leonardo Di Caprio is a massive art lover, and even has an original Picasso in his personal collection.

Other celebs with major art collections include Pharrell Williams, Beyonce and Jay-Z, the Beckhams, Elton John and loads more!

ANDY WARHOL

Andy Warhol was an American artist who worked in a visual style called "pop art". He also had a fascinating life!

Andy Warhol's real surname was "Warhola". After seeing his name misspelled by accident, he liked it so much he decided to keep it.

His mum was an artist too – and she taught him to draw while recovering from a childhood illness.

One of his most famous pieces was *Campbell's Soup Cans* – which showed loads of repeated pictures of cans of soup!

He also created portraits of famous faces of his time, including Hollywood actress Marilyn Monroe. Warhol also became a big celebrity in his own right!

Warhol would often change his date of birth whenever asked about it.

He made over 60 films – one of which was a six-hour recording of his friend sleeping!

He was a hypochondriac – which means he often thought he was seriously ill, even when he wasn't. He was also scared of doctors and hospitals!

Every month, Warhol would seal a different item inside a box to create a time capsule. Items he sealed up included a mummified foot, a silver belt buckle and a pile of Christmas wrapping paper.

He survived a murder attempt by the author Valerie Solanas, who shot him at his studio in New York.

TERRIFIC TECH

Art isn't just about simple paint and canvas – you can also use all sorts of modern day tech.

Kelly Richardson is an artist who creates entire landscapes using HD video and projections. The results range from holographic trees to amazing raining fireballs.

Love playing video games? Hooray! You're already an art fan. In 2011, the Smithsonian American Art Museum held an exhibition of images from throughout the history of gaming, called *The Art of Video Games*.

If you're a football fan you might have seen some impressive art mown into football pitches. Leicester City's groundsman John Ledwidge gained fame for the awesome patterns he cut into the grass at the club's stadium. Since 2017, however, England's Premier League has placed a ban on fancy pitch patterns.

First published 2019 by order of the Tate Trustees
by Tate Publishing, a division of Tate Enterprises Ltd,
Millbank, London SW1P 4RG

www.tate.org.uk/publishing

Text and artwork © Gary Panton
First published 2019

A catalogue record for this book is available from the British Library

ISBN 978 1 84976 661 6

Distributed in the United States and Canada by ABRAMS, New York
Library of Congress Control Number applied for
Printed and bound in China by Toppan Leefung Co. Ltd